21st-Century
Engineering Solutions
for Climate Change

DROUGHTS AND CROP FAILURE

KAITLYN DULING

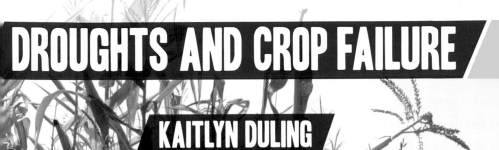

Cavendish
Square
New York

Published in 2019 by Cavendish Square Publishing, LLC
243 5th Avenue, Suite 136, New York, NY 10016

Website: cavendishsq.com

This publication represents the opinions and views of the author based on his or her personal
experience, knowledge, and research. The information in this book serves as a general
guide only. The author and publisher have used their best efforts in preparing this book and
disclaim liability rising directly or indirectly from the use and application of this book.

All websites were available and accurate when this book was sent to press.

Library of Congress Cataloging-in-Publication Data

Names: Duling, Kaitlyn, author.
Title: Droughts and crop failure / Kaitlyn Duling.
Description: First edition. | New York : Cavendish Square, 2019. |
Series: 21st-century engineering solutions for climate change |
Includes bibliographical references and index.
Identifiers: LCCN 2018004034 (print) | LCCN 2018006695 (ebook) |
ISBN 9781502638373 (ebook) | ISBN 9781502638359 (library bound) |
ISBN 9781502638366 (pbk.)
Subjects: LCSH: Droughts--Juvenile literature. | Crop losses--Juvenile literature.
Classification: LCC QC929.25 (ebook) |
LCC QC929.25.D85 2019 (print) | DDC 363.34/929--dc23
LC record available at https://lccn.loc.gov/2018004034

Editorial Director: David McNamara
Editor: Kristen Susienka
Copy Editor: Rebecca Rohan
Associate Art Director: Amy Greenan
Designer: Alan Sliwinski/Megan Mette
Production Coordinator: Karol Szymczuk
Photo Research: J8 Media

The photographs in this book are used by permission and through the courtesy of: Cover Bibiphoto/Shutterstock.com; p. 4
Ardni/Shutterstock.com; p. 6 Gustavo Izus Anella Reta Christopher Huffaker/AFP/Newscom; p. 8 George Rose/Getty Images;
p. 14 Angela N Perryman/Shutterstock.com; p. 16 Catalin Petolea/Shutterstock.com; p. 18 John Saeki Laurence Chu/AFP/
Newscom; ; p. 22 John Moore/Getty Images; p. 26 Romolo Tavani/Shutterstock.com; p. 29 Simon Maina/AFP/Getty Images;
p. 30 Rodger Bosch/AFP/Getty Images; p. 32 Farooq Naeem/AFP/Getty Images; p. 34 VCG/Getty Images; p. 36 Travis Heying/
Wichita Eagle/TNS/Getty Images; p. 38 Seth Perlman/AP Images; p. 40 Photographyfirm/Shutterstock.com; p. 43 Andrey_Popov/
Shutterstock.com; p. 45 Courtesy FLUID; p. 48 Kekyalyaynen/Shutterstock.com; p. 51 Bruce C. Murray/Shutterstock.com; p.
55 DumbTube/Alamy Stock Photo; p. 61 Ernesto Benavides/AFP/Getty Images; p. 65 Fred the Oyster/Wikimedia Commons/
File:Atmospheric Water Generator diagram.svg/CC BY SA 4.0; p. 69 Deon Raath/Foto24/Gallo Images/Getty Images.

Printed in the United States of America

CONTENTS

CHAPTER ONE

WHAT IS DROUGHT, ANYWAY?

Some weather disasters are easy to predict. Everyone knows when a hurricane is coming or when a snowstorm is about to hit. The aftermath of a tornado is clear. A flood can devastate an area for a long time. However, other types of weather events sneak up on you. A drought is one example. Drought is the absence of water. It can start slowly, with a gradual loss in precipitation before an area enters a long, dry period. It can also happen suddenly, hitting

Opposite: During a drought, everything dries up, including the soil.

a region with a lack of water and ending just as rapidly as it began. A drought can affect a community, city, state, or entire region in several different ways. The economy, public health, and agriculture can be affected, among many other things.

Types of Drought

There are three main types of drought that deal directly with precipitation. It is important to have a basic understanding of them in order to investigate the specific type of climate change–directed drought that is happening across the world today, and how that is affecting crops, animals, humans, and even the climate itself.

This drought map shows the various levels of severity that can occur.

Meteorological and Climatological Drought

Sometimes, dry weather simply dominates a given area. Scientists have an understanding of the "normal," or baseline, amount of moisture in the air, soil, and bodies of water. These statistics have been derived from decades of careful study. When the degree of dryness as well as the length of dryness reaches a certain point relative to the average figures, scientists would refer to this as meteorological drought.

In some parts of the world, the word "drought" is only used after a certain number of days without precipitation. The moisture levels in Florida are different from those in India, and those in France, and Antarctica, and so on. Therefore, there is no single number or figure that marks the threshold for referring to conditions as "drought." This is decided on a case-by-case basis. We can compare this to a tornado. It is easy to look at a certain swirling cloud formation and wind speed and name something a tornado. Droughts are trickier. Some places have lots of rainfall, like the Pacific Northwest in the United States, parts of Brazil, and London, England. Other places have hardly any rainfall: US deserts and parts of Australia and Africa. The regular climate and precipitation pattern in a specific place will determine what a drought looks like there. This is sometimes referred to as climatological drought.

Hydrological Drought

The second type of drought is hydrological. The term "hydro" refers to water. That's an easy way to remember what this type of drought deals with—a change in water supply. Scientists can identify hydrological drought by low water levels in lakes, rivers, and reservoirs, as well as reduced flow in streams and even decreased snowpack in areas with significant snow on the ground. Usually, an area will

This photo shows historically low water levels in California's Lake Shasta, a reservoir that feeds the Sacramento River.

first experience meteorological drought, with its decreased rainfall, and then the signs of hydrological drought will start to show. This type of drought can affect the water that we use to drink, irrigate farms, and bathe. It takes a long time for a drought to become hydrological, and it also takes a long time for an area to recover from this type.

Agricultural Drought

When meteorological and hydrological drought occur together, the characteristics link to form agricultural drought, which highlights the effects on crops, livestock, forestry, and more. These types of droughts tend to be short-term and are characterized by insufficient soil moisture. Dry soil can cause massive decreases in crop growth and production. Put simply, crops fail when we are unable to meet plant water demands. For farmers, especially in times of drought, irrigation is not always an option. If it is not addressed quickly and during critical periods of growth, drought can severely harm crop production. Though these periods tend to be short, they can have lasting impacts on industries, land areas for future growth, and the health and wellness of people who rely on locally-grown food.

Drought and Climate Change

What are the causes of these three types of drought? Drier-than-normal conditions can and do occur at regular intervals across our globe. This is natural. There are dry times and wet times. However, over the last several decades, periods of drought have become longer and more severe. This is thanks, in part, to climate change. The term "climate change" refers to changes in global and regional climate patterns. Climate is more than just rain. It includes temperatures, precipitation of all kinds, air pressure, and more. Scientists report that climate change has been occurring since about the mid-to-late twentieth century due to—at least in part—an increase in average atmospheric temperature. This is called global warming. Global warming has some natural causes, but it is often attributed to measurable increased levels of carbon dioxide and other "greenhouse gases" in Earth's atmosphere. These gases are produced by using fossil fuels—coal or gas burned to power cars, trucks, factories, and homes.

Scientists are beginning to link drought with climate change in concrete ways. As more and more greenhouse gases are released, the atmospheric temperature rises at all levels, including in the air closest to Earth's surface. As the air temperature increases, moisture evaporates from bodies of water. Lakes, rivers, and even the land all lose water to the air. As droughts become more common and harsher, recovery becomes harder too. Very dry soils are less able to absorb rainfall following a period of drought.

DID YOU KNOW?

The US Drought Monitor map was created in August 1999. It communicates the location and intensity of drought to the public, as well as to decision makers. Drought experts appreciate this simple, accurate way to see and consider drought conditions. The map includes six levels of intensity, as well as short- and long-term impact areas. Canada has its own national drought monitor as well.

This can lead to floods in agricultural fields, which harms crop growth.

Unfortunately, climate scientists don't see any indications that global warming will slow down or stop anytime soon. According to NASA, 2016 was the warmest year on record, and 2017 was only slightly cooler. As long as climate change continues, the world will experience more droughts, and for longer periods of time. Meteorological and hydrological droughts will necessarily cause agricultural droughts, which, in turn, will cause socioeconomic droughts. This final type of drought is marked by changes in the supply and demand of economic goods such as food, water, and energy. In a socioeconomic drought, demand will outstrip supply. This can create stress on the little water that is still available. This type is slow to occur, but once a community faces socioeconomic drought, it is incredibly difficult to recover.

Today, drought is occurring in many parts of the world. In the United States, most of the state of California has been under drought for the past few years, and the conditions show few signs of changing. Nevada, Oregon, and other western states frequently

WHAT SKEPTICS SAY

Not everyone agrees with scientists' assessments about the relationship between global warming and drought. Some people believe that droughts—even their recent increase in length and severity—can be attributed to natural climate cycles.

In the United States, drought conditions have been extremely varied since 1895, when official recordkeeping began. This statistic is what many skeptics point to when they claim that droughts are naturally occurring. What's more, according to the Environmental Protection Agency (EPA, a federal government agency), the last fifty years have been wetter than average across the United States. New indexes are being developed and tested to better measure conditions in specific regions, but they haven't been used long enough to see concrete results.

experience drought as well. In Canada, lower Saskatchewan is often affected. Kenya, South Africa, and India have recently come into devastating periods of drought that will probably continue, on and off, in future years and decades. As these areas continue to deal with a lack of moisture and precipitation, it is likely that they will experience agricultural issues and crop failure, which could easily lead to socioeconomic drought situations.

Developing countries are especially at risk when it comes to droughts affecting supply and demand. This is unlike California, which is hard hit by drought but will likely not experience famine anytime soon. Famine is the widespread scarcity of food, and it

Droughts make it harder for wild animals, like this hippo in South Africa, to find the water needed to live and thrive.

is often influenced by crop failure. Ultimately, as global warming spreads and intensifies its hold on the planet, more and more people could be facing the realities of extreme drought and famine.

With the knowledge of what causes drought conditions, it is important to assess today's conditions and make a plan for the future. Many scientists and engineers are already working on ways to combat the disturbing trends and conditions seen across the world each day.

DID YOU KNOW?

As the climate heats up and droughts become more frequent, some communities are adversely affected more than others. Pastoral groups have been some of the hardest hit. These communities consist of people who travel and subsist through gathering, selling, foraging, and short-term farming. Long-term drought conditions in places like Northern Kenya have exhausted the coping strategies of such groups, since they depend so heavily on the availability of natural resources such as water.

CHAPTER TWO

DROUGHT AND CROP FAILURE TODAY

If current trends in fossil fuel usage are not slowed or reversed, it is likely that Earth's atmosphere will continue to warm, creating climate change conditions on the ground. A warming planet will create more droughts and will cause drought periods to last longer. Today, some parts of the world naturally experience more drought and near-drought conditions than others. However, over time, those areas will expand and drought will enter regions where it has not

Opposite: When drought occurs in the American Midwest, crops like this corn suffer.

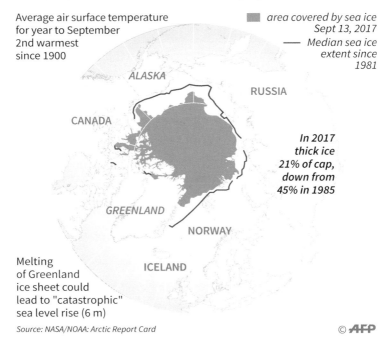

Warming Arctic affects world weather
Linked to extreme weather in North America, say scientists

Average air surface temperature for year to September 2nd warmest since 1900

▇ *area covered by sea ice Sept 13, 2017*

—— *Median sea ice extent since 1981*

ALASKA

RUSSIA

CANADA

In 2017 thick ice 21% of cap, down from 45% in 1985

GREENLAND

NORWAY

ICELAND

Melting of Greenland ice sheet could lead to "catastrophic" sea level rise (6 m)

Source: NASA/NOAA: Arctic Report Card

© **AFP**

This map explores the Arctic sea ice melt, and how it could affect sea levels and weather across the globe in the future.

previously occurred. Scientists are able to predict these conditions using advanced climate models, tools that build on historical data to take a look at what our future could hold. These models suggest that if human behavior stays constant, warmer, drier times will be expected across Earth in the years ahead. Some people might think, "So what? I'd love to live in a warmer climate! Bring on the ice cream and the suntan!" However, a hot and dry climate doesn't just mean an excuse to break out the sunglasses. It can have disastrous effects on energy, ecosystems, transportation, water supply, health, and agriculture.

Long-Term Effects of Drought

Remember the phrase "agricultural drought?" This refers to the ways in which droughts affect livestock and crops. Almost 40 percent of the people in the world rely financially on agriculture. This is where 1.3 billion people get their main income. A farmer's worst nightmare is something called crop failure. This refers to a failure of crops (like corn, beans, sugar, or apples) to yield a sufficient supply in order to feed a community and/or provide a surplus of product to sell for money. For farmers in America and Canada, growing enough to make money is usually the biggest issue. On large-scale farms in North America, huge swaths of acreage produce corn and soybeans, not to eat but to use in livestock feed, biofuel, and other products that ultimately aren't consumed by humans. Here, farmers depend on surplus crops to sell to other industries. In other countries, such as those in South America or Africa, families own subsistence farms. This type of farm is self-sufficient: farmers grow just enough food to feed themselves, their families, and perhaps other members of their local community. There is little or no selling of crops. For both large-scale farmers and those who live off of what they grow, crop failure is no joke. It can mean a lack of income or even a lack of food to eat. Without these basic necessities, it becomes difficult for people to survive and thrive.

Drought and crop failure aren't limited events that start and stop. Drought has a slow start, can last for years, and then affects the land for a long time after the rains have finally begun to fall. Just like extremely wet conditions and floods can adversely affect soil, drought puts stress on the land in ways that not only make the ground "thirsty," but ultimately change the physical, chemical, and biological activities that occur in the soil. From the most basic standpoint, a lack of water means that plants cannot take in the nutrients they need in order to survive. As the soil dries up and its temperature increases, the microbial activities and nutrient processing that a plant goes through are negatively impacted, increasing the release of carbon dioxide and nitrate into the soil system. Altogether, the chemical makeup and nutrient cycling of the plants and soil are forced to change, and those changes are not for the better. When a drought causes crop failure, it does much more than dry up the plants. It affects the microscopic activities that are constantly occurring underground, throughout the soil, and within the roots and bodies of plants. What does or does not happen at that level can cause crops to fail season after season, long past the time when conditions were considered drought-like.

Drought in North America

Historically, the United States, as well as the whole of North America, has been susceptible to drought. The Dust Bowl of the 1930s is one example. During the Dust Bowl, the prairies of the American and Canadian plains were so stricken with drought that severe dust storms ravaged the areas, bringing high wind speeds and dust that choked people and livestock. Crop failure was abundant, as overproduction and a

Ranches and farms can be crippled when droughts dry up their pasturelands. This cow is on land in Colorado in 2012.

lack of rain killed the crops that normally kept soil in place. For decades, 1934 was known as the hottest year on record. (This changed in 2014.) During the dust storms, wind lifted the soil off the ground into enormous clouds of dust that traveled as far away as Washington, DC. It wasn't until the early 1940s that rain returned to normal levels. Some argue that parts of the Midwest still have not fully recovered from the Dust Bowl.

Today, droughts of this magnitude are not unheard of. In 2012, the US Department of Agriculture declared a natural disaster in 2,245 counties due to severe drought. Those counties cover 71 percent of the United States. That year, drought created devastating conditions across the southern, midwestern, and western United States, as well as central and eastern Canada and parts of Mexico. How could something this catastrophic happen? To some, the causes were natural. To others, global warming was a huge player in the game. The winter of 2011–2012 saw very few winter storms and very little winter precipitation. That meant in spring, there was very little snow to melt, evaporate, and create rainfall. Conditions remained dry for months. That summer, a major heat wave merged with the dry conditions to further evaporate groundwater, rivers, lakes, and reservoirs. The soil hardened. The rain did not fall. Temperatures were

/ DID YOU KNOW? /

In times of drought, areas become more susceptible to wildfires. Less soil moisture and dry vegetation, matched with hotter, drier weather, means that fires can be more frequent and more devastating. In 2017, following years of drought, unprecedented wildfires raged across California.

high and climbing higher. The summer of 2012 was one of the worst heat waves in North American history.

As the drought continued, wildfires ravaged the forests of Colorado. In California, the drought blocked off the mouths of rivers with sandbars, which prevented fish from reaching their spawning grounds. The harvest of salmon and other fish was extremely low due to the lack of rainfall. In the Midwest, crops failed. There was simply not enough water for plants to drink, and the intense heat dried up everything. Corn, wheat, and soybean farmers in Illinois, Indiana, and other states were stuck with crops that were unsalvageable. While a portion of the crops might still be good, they had to weigh the pros and cons—was one-third of the crop enough to justify the high bill for using a combine?

One way that farmers dealt with the lack of sellable crops was to sell off their livestock. In fact, in order to deal with the sudden influx of meat into the market, the US Department of Defense bought up meat at low prices, stockpiling for the years ahead. Meanwhile, corn and soybean prices climbed higher as supply grew thin. When crop prices soar, that means eventual higher prices for milk, poultry, beef, and pork for consumers. Then there are the African and Latin American countries that depend on imported grains from North America. They also felt the "heat" from the 2012 drought, though they felt it more financially than in temperature. In situations like these, experts fear food riots and other forms of social disruption due simply to a lack of affordable food.

The 2012 drought saw other casualties across the agricultural industry: farmers killed off pigs and cows rather than pay for the high-priced corn to feed them. Horse rescue shelters saw an increase in the number of abandoned horses due to high prices for horse feed. Biofuel plants that produce ethanol for automobiles had to slow or, in some cases, even halt production for a period of time because corn prices grew too high to manage. Sales of lawn mowers and tractors almost halted altogether. Farmers began to borrow more money, putting stress onto banking institutions and making the market more unstable. In the midst of the 2012 drought, experts predicted that price shocks wouldn't really come until the following winter and spring, especially in developing countries that depended on imports. They were right. A bad drought doesn't just dry up crops, it affects the entire global economy.

Drought Across the Globe

In recent years, research has shown that the countries that will be most affected by climate change and drought are those that do the least to contribute to emissions and global warming. The principle of common but differentiated responsibilities calls on wealthy countries that emit the majority of greenhouse gases to do more to address global

This globe tries to illustrate global warming. Warmth and dry temperatures can be felt across the entire planet.

DROUGHT IN ANCIENT TIMES

In the Bible, drought is mentioned at least ten times in the Old Testament and several more times in the New Testament. According to ancient documents like the Bible, severe droughts and famine fell on those living in ancient Israel. For the Hebrews, drought was seen as a punishment from God.

Today, archaeologists are studying cliff sediments that go back seventy thousand years, and they are able to detect dark and light bands of earth that mark both wet and dry times. Scientists are also able to use sediment cores from the floor of the Dead Sea to note times of drought and rainfall hundreds of thousands of years ago.

warming. It places less responsibility on developing countries that have, historically, emitted fewer greenhouse gases. Developing countries, too, are more vulnerable to rising sea levels, drought, crop failure, and other issues. Droughts are a global phenomenon—they affect people everywhere. The impacts of drought vary from region to region, but the least-developed countries suffer the worst. In these areas, communities experience adverse effects on their health, water sources, power generation, income, and food security. These countries are more susceptible to adverse conditions during drought times, as well as less prepared to recover fully from extreme drought.

Kenya

The Kenyan drought began in the autumn of 2016, when unusually high temperatures mixed with a lack of rainfall. Northwest and Southeast Kenya were particularly affected by low rainfall. The government declared a national drought emergency, specifically focused on food insecurity. This refers to the condition in which people do not have reliable access to enough affordable, nutritious food. According to the United Nations, waterholes and rivers dried up across the country, which led to crop failure and livestock depletion. As noted above, when farmers have low crop yields, they are often forced to sell or kill their livestock. Additionally, if there isn't enough food or water for humans, there isn't enough for animals either, and many die naturally. Now, the prices of basic staples such as maize flour and sugar are increasing by huge percentages as supply declines. As prices climb, the availability of basic commodities goes down, even for water.

Frustrated by widespread drought, residents took to the streets of Nairobi, Kenya, in 2015 to demand action on climate change.

The drought and lack of food have become political issues—citizens are blaming President Uhuru Kenyatta for his lack of response to the drought. In response, the government has been importing sugar, corn, milk, and other necessities. It has also allocated some food aid in order to help hungry families.

South Africa

In South Africa, much of the region has been in recovery from drought conditions that hit in the last few years, but the city of Cape Town, on the tip of the African continent, experienced its worst drought in over a century in 2018. That year, it came

In 2018, people in South Africa collected limited amounts of water each week for drinking, cooking, and cleaning.

close to hitting "Day Zero," the day on which water taps in homes run completely dry. For three years previously, the city experienced extremely low rainfall, which resulted in low water in the dams. In order to conserve water, the city banned car washing and the filling of swimming pools. Residents' water usage was restricted, and all were strongly urged to use as little water as possible. The shortage of water had ill effects on farmers of peaches, wheat, grapes, and sheep. Growers of wine-grapes were unable to meet their plants' demands, which was frustrating due to the fact that South Africa is the world's ninth-largest wine exporter.

Pakistan

Some countries might seem like surprising homes for droughts because they also regularly experience monsoon seasons. But a season doesn't stick around forever. When the monsoons don't provide enough rain, Pakistan is left dry. Recently, the Pakistan Council of Research in Water Sources forecasted that the country will face "absolute scarcity" level by 2025. Unlike Cape Town, Pakistan's largest city, Karachi,

In Pakistan, water shortages in 2010 forced residents to carefully fill jugs and buckets at a communal filling point.

has not instituted water policies in order to curb use. The country, which is dependent on water from the Indus River basin, has the world's fourth-largest rate of water usage. Poor water management, population growth, urban development, and climate change are all factors helping to increase Pakistan's dangerous and growing lack of water.

India

Pakistan isn't the only country that has been impacted by monsoon rain. Over three hundred million people in India are currently experiencing drought conditions following two years of sparse rain. In rural areas, the situation is decidedly grim. The lands have dried up completely, and those who previously farmed are being forced to travel to find both food and work. The drought in India has been caused by a combination of factors: poor water conservation, a lack of effective water policy, two years of slow monsoon rains, and a massive 2016 heat wave that shut down schools and resulted in thousands of deaths. For farmers, the unending drought means unpaid debts, medical issues, extreme hunger, and very little hope. Without aid, those living in rural areas will only lose what little access to water they currently have.

/ DID YOU KNOW? /

For over one thousand years, people in western India have been utilizing stepwells (*baolis* in Hindi) to harvest the small amounts of rain the desert regions receive. These reservoirs are built into the earth to provide water for drinking and farming. A circular well pulls groundwater up from the bottom and rainwater collects at the top. People reach the water by descending the steps.

China

Farmers in rural China have been dealing with a long-term water crisis for years. Drought has been helping to dry up over half of the country's significant rivers, causing groundwater levels to hit major lows. In some provinces, recent years have seen car washes and bathhouses close due to lack of water. For farmers living in those areas, yields have shrunk considerably, and the federal government has decided to rely more heavily on imports of water-heavy foods like grains and vegetable oil. In addition to drought and warm temperatures, the country has seen what remains of their water used up by industries in the northeast. Steel

In 2013, farmers in drought-ravaged China struggled to keep livestock alive.

foundries, coal-fired power plants, and factories have not only hogged much-needed water, but pollution and chemical runoff from the industrial sector has contaminated 60 percent of China's groundwater. The combined effects of nature and people are ensuring that China will have water scarcity problems well into the future.

Putting the Problem Pieces Together

Droughts do much more than dry up puddles and cause farmers to rely on irrigation. They can, in fact, bring entire industries to their knees. When a drought turns from meteorological to hydrological, and then becomes agricultural in nature, across-the-board failures in all types of crops occur. This can happen to grapes in California, wheat in South Africa, corn in Indiana, and other foods that are grown throughout the world. When crops fail, farmers suffer. Sometimes this means subsistence farmers are forced to move away from their homes, finding jobs in cities or becoming traveling hunter-gatherers. In other places, industrial farmers might sell off their livestock, flooding the market with cheap meat while grain, produce, and milk prices soar. Years later, the prices of meat will remain unstable as the market waits to recover from the unnatural influx.

At the same time, communities experiencing a lack of water for crops may find that there is little to no water for basic needs such as cleaning, drinking, bathing, and swimming. Rivers may run low and dry, halting boat transportation, which can be especially disruptive in regions where waterways are utilized as the main thoroughfares. This might seem like a foreign practice, but within the United States, grains are frequently moved over water. The drought of 2012 had such a negative effect on the

Farmers are some of the first people affected when drought conditions occur in an area.

Mississippi River watershed that barge traffic was cut, the amount of goods carried down the river was drastically reduced, and Americans working in the tugboat industry suddenly found themselves out of work. Of course, the post-drought situation was hardly better—flooding in the Mississippi River area the following spring caused barge traffic disruptions, even further reducing the ability of farmers to get their grains into international hands. Global food prices were sent on a rollercoaster ride. International prices soared, and domestic prices followed suit. Additionally, leaders feared the crises of national security and humanitarian issues that could occur with a continued lack of food to be imported into foreign nations. Today, slow recovery efforts continue.

Where hydroelectric power is abundant, low water levels can mean a crunch on electricity production. All of these factors can result in stresses to a community's socioeconomic fabric. When people lose their means of income and cannot access basic necessities such as food, water, and power, a community suffers. The reverberations of socioeconomic drought in one town or village can be felt further out, especially when it

On the Mississippi River, boats have a hard time moving through water when the water is low.

comes to a lack of important exports, the closing of a waterway, or a rapidly spreading wildfire. Drought can cause great harm to communities both small and large. Whole countries can be devastated by years of overpowering heat and insufficient rainfall. This is why it is so important to develop and implement management practices and solutions that can help to ease the effects of drought, and potentially prevent them. Only then can the world's citizens get a small reprieve from this ancient plague that occurs more frequently, and for longer periods, as the years pass by.

OLD SOLUTIONS TO NEW PROBLEMS

For hundreds of years, the Native American tribe of North Fork Mono has been thinning the forests in the Sierra Nevada mountains. They do this to save water and prevent forest fires. Today, they are working with the US Forest Service to use these ancient techniques to make sure that forests have the water they need. Tree and shrub removal ensures that snowmelt seeps into aquifers instead of being consumed by plants. Less brush also means less chance of wildfires. One study from the University of California suggests that thinning the forests could add up to 16 percent more water flow out of the Sierra Nevada, redirecting it to the state's water supply and helping to prevent fires at the same time.

CHAPTER THREE

MODERN AND FUTURE TECH

I n the coming years and decades, global warming will surely continue to have an impact on our planet. More countries are developing full-fledged industrial sectors, experiencing population growth, and urbanizing their communities, all of which results in the burning of more fossil fuels. Though some policies are in effect and a few strides have even been made toward global energy policies, the fact remains that the climate is currently changing. Shifting weather

Opposite: Farms will continue to be negatively affected by droughts unless we come up with some efficient solutions.

patterns and hotter temperatures will continue to mean more drought. How can we cope? Certainly there are solutions outside of slathering on the sunscreen and waiting until water supplies run out. Industry leaders, innovators, students, policymakers, and others are all working toward new technologies and fresh answers to water issues. The faster these dreams can become a reality, the better.

Water Monitoring

For now, it is a fact that drought will continue to affect the earth in the future, especially if behaviors don't drastically change. So, many people are working on solutions that will help individuals, communities, cities, and entire regions become more resilient to the effects of drought.

One of the best ways to build up resilience to drought is to have water-monitoring systems in place. In many developed towns and urban areas, water is already monitored for quality. It is tested on a regular basis to make sure it is safe for consumption. When the water in a local system is not safe to ingest, a town might issue a boil order or alert citizens to unsafe levels of chemicals, bacteria, or other unsavory things in the water. During a boil order, residents are advised to boil their tap water before consuming it to avoid potential contamination. This is important work, but the amount of available water is another critical piece of information. The public is often unaware of how much water is available—and even where it comes from. The water people drink might come from an aquifer underground, a moving body of water such as a river, or elsewhere. Water can be sourced from city water supplies, surface water (wetland, lake, ocean), ground water (wells or aquifers), or rainwater collected and stored by a family, business, or organization.

Many everyday household tasks use large amounts of water, such as running a dishwasher or clothes washer.

Monitoring water use over a period of time, with the regular collection of data, will provide information on how much is used from different sources, and it will allow the identification of inefficiencies in that system or the ability to set reasonable targets for reduction of water use. In the future, reduction of water use will be a critical piece of the drought puzzle, be it in local homes or on large-scale industrial levels.

There are already sources of real-time data when it comes to measuring water usage. Tools like WaterSignal attach to a property's water meter to give up-to-the-hour data about water usage, costs, evaporation, and leaks. A solution like this offers many benefits. For a business, it can help to attain the LEED certification given by the US Green Building Council, which measures sustainability factors in buildings. Water data also helps to create benchmarks for usage, such as an accurate baseline and then goals for reducing water consumption. Products that alert owners to leaks help to stop loss of water more efficiently than ever before.

While WaterSignal is geared toward businesses and corporate buildings, products like FLUID aim to make water monitoring the norm in everyday households. FLUID snaps around the main water pipe in a house, connects to Wi-Fi, and syncs to an app on a smartphone or tablet. The device uses ultrasonic technology to measure the water flowing through the pipes. The app gives yearly, monthly, weekly, and even daily data about how much water is being used—and exactly where that water is going. It breaks the sources down. A certain percentage of water at home goes toward showering, while another part is used in the dishwasher, toilet, lawn sprinkler, and so on. FLUID also works on a consumer level by measuring the water in gallons, rather than in the units that usually show up on a utility bill. Units don't mean

Tools like FLUID help everyday consumers monitor their water usage.

much to the average person, but gallons are easy to visualize. The average American consumes between 80 and 100 gallons (303 to 379 liters) of water each day! Canada is second only to the United States. Canadians consume around 86 gallons (326 L) a day.

Once water usage has been measured, what is the next step? In order to ensure that drought doesn't take the worst possible toll and that there will be enough water to go around, it is important for people to conserve water as much as possible. Some water conservation tactics are extremely easy, such as installing a water-saving showerhead or low-flow faucet. Water leaks can be noted and fixed, especially when using monitoring technology like WaterSignal or FLUID. There are also behavior-based changes that individuals and companies can make, such as shorter showers, full loads of laundry and dishes, and being extremely mindful of how long the water is running during activities such as brushing teeth and washing vegetables. Individuals can also think big about water—every time people use electricity, energy and water are being expended in power plants, not to mention all the fossil fuels that are being released into the atmosphere, adding to global warming and increasing the chance of drought. Once people start noticing their water usage and working to decrease it, it will become habit, almost like a game: What little changes can you make to reduce water consumption in your home or school? How can you encourage others to reduce their water consumption too?

Landscape and Stormwater Solutions

When the drought ends and the rain finally falls, where does it all end up? One of the ways in which governments at both local and state levels can ensure hydrological health in their urban communities is to invest in "green" infrastructure for water management. Additionally, individuals and families can take steps to design their own properties to facilitate sustainable movement and storage of rain and snowmelt. Thinking about resilience to droughts shouldn't happen during the middle of a dry period. Those thoughts and discussions need to begin during times of wet weather, which can be seasons that offer all sorts of community benefits.

Traditional storm-water management moves precipitation away from homes and businesses through sewers, gutters, pipes, and drainage systems that pour storm water into water treatment plants. There are benefits to this type of system, as storm-water runoff can carry elements like garbage and bacteria away from city centers. However, heavy rain can result in erosion and flooding in urban streams.

Today, there are many options for green infrastructure that allows soil and plants to naturally absorb, filter, and manage the rain that falls. A series of natural areas can help to create a healthier urban environment that includes flood protection, cleaner

Water treatment plants are one option for curbing our water use.

water, habitats for natural animals and plants, and even cleaner air. When cities adopt green infrastructure, they are better able to build resiliency to drought and can help to avoid water shortages that put industries, farmers, and citizens in danger. Some simple examples of green infrastructure solutions include:

- Rainwater harvesting: Collecting and storing rainfall can be particularly helpful in extremely dry and arid places where water is already in limited supply. People can use a rain barrel outside of their homes, but these can also be used on corporate buildings, schools, offices, and almost anywhere that qualifies as a building.
- Planter boxes: These are the small green spaces seen in and around sidewalks in urban areas. They collect and absorb rain from sidewalks and parking lots. They also provide beauty to the streetscape.

- Permeable pavement: Porous asphalt and interlocking paving stones have been gaining popularity in recent years. These are surfaces that filter and store rainwater right where it falls. They can be used as sidewalk and road materials instead of traditional, non-pervious concrete.

- "Green" roofs: What if, instead of blank roofs that do nothing but absorb sunlight, buildings had roofs covered in plants? These roofs do actually exist! They help filter rainfall, look beautiful, and aid in the absorption of carbon dioxide from the air, slowing global warming.

- Rain gardens: A rain garden is simple to grow and easy to enjoy. Installed almost anywhere, shallow garden basins are ideal for collecting runoff from sidewalks, streets, and rooftops. Through natural rain gardens, water gets infiltrated and evaporated all on its own.

Green choices don't just fall to large-scale urban landscape design. Personal property can be landscaped for resilience to droughts as well. There are many simple and affordable ways for people to "go green" in their own yards. First things first— they can stop watering their lawns! Many people are tempted to bring the hose out to water their front yards and create lush grass yards, but that does not have to be the norm. There are many grass alternatives with which one can cover and decorate the front and backyard areas of the home. For homeowners who do water their grass, each square foot of grass removed can save at least 44 gallons (167 L) of water a year.

There are many grass alternatives that homeowners can choose in order to save water. This lawn is an example of xeriscaping.

In fact, some utility companies in California have been offering rebates to customers who replace their lawns with drought-resistant plants and water-saving features. When a person conserves water through creative landscaping, the process is referred to as xeriscaping. The options for grass alternatives abound.

Synthetic grass, more commonly known as turf or astroturf, was a popular option when it first appeared on sports fields in the 1960s, and today some homeowners still utilize this "fake grass." Turf comes with its own bucket of concerns about the chemicals present in its material, its softness, and how hot it gets under the sun. But it can be affordable, and following installation, it is nearly maintenance-free.

Another non-plant option is groundcover, which could include anything from small rocks to mulch to crushed shells or even sand. Yards decorated with groundcover have their own quiet sense of peace and can be quite decorative and beautiful. Homeowners can also try a mix of paving stones and drought-tolerant plants like lavender, sage, and lantana.

What if people still want plants in their yards? That's OK! Using native plants that naturally occur in a region and have adapted to the local weather is key. These should require little to no watering. As a bonus, they provide habitats for insects, birds, and small animals. Shrubs, trees, and certain grasses are native to various regions. Online tools exist to find out which plants are native to different communities. In any region, desert plants are a healthy choice, as they consume very little water. When kept in pots, cacti and succulents can be used to decorate a yard in almost any climate.

Answers for Agriculture

As discussed, there are many ways to combat drought and build resilience, including reducing overall energy

DID YOU KNOW?

A new app is helping utility companies introduce their customers to more water-friendly habits. "Dropcountr" sends automated leak alerts to customers, as well as monthly usage reports so families can track their water usage. Homeowners can track water consumption on a weekly, daily, or even hourly basis!

consumption, reducing water usage, investing in green infrastructure, and rethinking the way properties are landscaped. One of the biggest dangers of drought, however, is how it can negatively affect crops and our food supply. Water scarcity and the prevalence of drought are driving farmers and researchers to come up with new solutions to deal with drought.

One option is simply to plant different foods. In California, citrus and avocado growers are turning to other, less thirsty and more profitable crops like grapes. Vineyards require about 25 percent less water than citrus fruits such as oranges and grapefruits. The trend toward crop diversification isn't exactly new in California. In the past, it saw booms in the production of wheat and cotton, but they have since faded as new trends emerged.

Another solution taking hold in California, Spain, Italy, and other areas is called dry farming. This is simply a method that relies on seasonal rainfall and requires a particular and well-maintained relationship with the soil. A farmer must cultivate a layer of "dust mulch," which seals in moisture near the plant's roots. Those who stand by dry farming say that the

Dry farming is one method that grape farmers are utilizing at the Ghirardelli Vineyard in California.

unique method results in higher-quality food, such as wine grapes, even if the yield isn't as high. When the vines need to go in search of water, they put down extremely deep roots—sometimes as deep as 20 to 30 feet (6 to 9 meters)! This creates grapes that have deep flavor, rich smells, and characteristics of the land where they are grown. Almonds, which are California's second most valuable crop, use extreme amounts of water when they are grown on industrial farms. But a smaller area of land can be used to easily dry farm an almond crop.

In addition to choosing which crops to plant, farmers in dry areas are also taking a closer look at the soils in which they grow. No-till farming and cover cropping can both help to build healthier soil for almost any type of plant. In a no-till farming system, the soil does not get plowed under at the end of each season. Instead, the farmer plants new seeds directly onto last year's crop stubble. The old crop breaks down, creating mulch-like materials that help the soil to naturally retain moisture. Another option is to plant cover crops, like winter wheat and hairy vetch. These are not sold on the market but are grown in order to enhance and protect the soil. They do not deplete the soil; they retain water and add nutrients to the ground. According to the USDA, farmers who use cover crops have higher-than-average yields than those who do not. The USDA also reports that the benefit of cover crops can be even more pronounced in areas that are adversely affected by drought.

Across the globe, farmers are turning not only to different farming methods but also to more crops that are naturally drought-resistant. In Zimbabwe, maize has always been a natural staple, but it needs an ample amount of water to thrive. Now, as long midseason dry spells and frequent droughts change the climate of Zimbabwe, farmers are turning to plants like sorghum and millet. Crops like these are hardy and produce yields, though they may be small, during rainfall shortfalls. These alternative grains help to protect farmers from losing everything. If the maize crop fails or is too small, and farmers have no other crops to turn to, they will have to sell their livestock or move away from the farm and work in a city. When they grow at least some sorghum in addition to a maize crop, farmers have insured themselves against a fully failed season if the maize crop comes up empty. Similarly, farmers in semi-arid Kenya have begun to grow drought-resistant crops. Sorghum, millet, pigeon pea, cowpea, and green gram are increasingly popular choices.

While sorghum and other grains are naturally tough within drought conditions, scientists in the United States are also working to produce drought-resistant crops using genetic engineering. Plants that naturally tend to survive dry conditions have something called crassulacean acid metabolism, also known as CAM. Plants using CAM keep their leaves shut during the day, reducing evaporation of moisture, but open at night in order to collect carbon dioxide. These plants include prickly pear, pineapple, and vanilla orchids. One team of researchers believes they've found the genes that make up CAM, which could open the door to drought-specific genetic engineering of crops. These crops could be used to feed the growing global population or to power the world through biofuels. These scientists hope to engineer rice, wheat, soybeans and other plants to make them more adaptable to dry environments. Some of the biggest seed corporations have put big money into the genetic modification efforts. Monsanto, Syngenta, and DuPont have all invested.

In a less-invasive move, many companies are already conventionally breeding seeds to tolerate low-water levels. They are carefully bred to create seeds with the best gene patterns. For countries like Kenya and Zimbabwe, where these drought-resistant varieties could make a huge difference, the problems lie not in producing enough seeds but in distributing them. Many small-scale farmers don't have access

One way that buildings can become more "green" is to increase water efficiency. There are many strategies that support this. Efforts might include installing efficient plumbing fixtures, choosing locally adapted plants, and measuring water usage with a submeter.

to the seeds. Still others are deeply opposed to the new seeds, as they have to be repurchased every season instead of recycled year after year. Farmers don't want to lose control or financial stability in the battle to grow crops in regions that are becoming drier every year.

Unique Innovations

When it comes to battling drought and crop failure, agricultural solutions continue to gain steam, and the pressure to use less water increases. However, some people are taking a completely different route with the issue, coming up with truly unique innovations that could change the game on drought. Underground drilling, desalination, fog catching, cloud seeding, and atmospheric water generation are just some of the many ideas that may seem a little crazy at first, but might just be bold enough to work.

Desalination

Desalination is the process of turning seawater, or saltwater, into drinkable water. Unlike many drought solutions, desalination is not dependent on rain. It is already in use on many ships and submarines that operate in the planet's oceans. Though it sounds simple (just remove the salt and minerals, right?), desalination is much more expensive than extracting naturally fresh water from rivers or groundwater, recycling water, or conserving water. But as the worldwide water supply continues to become more depleted, desalination may be an option to be implemented on a larger scale. Already, over 20,000 desalination plants exist in 120 countries around the world. Florida, California, and Texas each have plants, though the largest users are the Middle East and North Africa. In early 2018, Saudi Arabia announced plans to spend

Nets like this one in Lima, Peru, can be used to catch water from fog.

over $500 million to build nine desalination plants on the coast of the Red Sea.

Fog Catching

Another technique aims to turn fog into drinking water. First devised in the 1980s, fog catching has gained popularity in various regions of the globe, including Chile, Ghana, Peru, and California, though none are yet producing enough to make a sizable contribution to water needs. The technology consists of a single- or double-layered mesh panel or "fog fence." Essentially, the nets act as collection areas for dew, just like one would see on blades of grass on an early spring morning. Through the natural process of condensation, water vapor in the atmosphere condenses into water droplets. A long collecting trough sits beneath the fog fence in order to catch the dew as it rolls down the panels. According to researchers, fog harvesting would work best in coastal areas that experience many long periods of fog. The world's largest fog-collection project is located in Marrakech, Morocco. It provides clean drinking water to five hundred people in five nearby villages that have been affected by droughts.

Drilling

Much of the water consumed in the United States is surface water—water collected from rivers, streams, and reservoirs. But when there isn't any surface water to be found, farmers turn to a hidden resource in the ground. Far below Earth's surface, the soil holds aquifers, areas full of water that has leaked down over the course of the last century. People have begun to dig into the soil to access these aquifers.

Due to the water's ancient history and the aggression with which it must be drilled, some people compare this method to drilling for oil or mining for

ANIMAL IMPACT

Drought not only affects people and their food supply—it adversely affects the fish, birds, wildlife, and insects that populate the world. Hydrological drought can destroy habitats like ponds, streams, and wetlands. When their homes dry up, animals may have no place to go. Drought doesn't just dry up the human food supply. It makes food and water harder to come by for animals, especially when many species are on the move due to lack of natural habitat. The reduction of food and water supply causes increased disease, forced migration, and eventually an increase in the number of species considered endangered, with the possibility of becoming extinct. The survival of many wild animals relies on human beings to keep the world a livable place for all living creatures.

coal. Once the water is gone, it's gone—and farmers aren't exactly slowing down. In California, ground drilling is highly unregulated, and each time one farmer drills for water, it drops the water table—the upper level of soil where rocks and earth are covered in water—even lower, forcing everyone to drill farther into the ground. Some go as far as 2,000 feet (610 m) under Earth's surface! As the water table sinks, the land sinks with it, damaging everything from roads to bridges to canals and more. They also use energy to drill the wells and pump the water. Since drilling is currently completely unregulated in California, there are no restrictions on how deep or how often a farmer can pump. Though legislation to regulate the practice is working its way through the state government, the state's aquifers may run out of water before there is any sort of policy change on ground drilling.

Atmospheric Water Generation

In many parts of the globe, water is not only scarce, but it is not suitable for drinking. In an effort to provide clean water to those who don't have reliable access to it, engineers have come up with systems to extract water from the air. Manufactured and sold by several different companies, atmospheric water generators are meant for homes or offices. Costing hundreds to thousands of dollars each, these machines work like extreme dehumidifiers. They chill the air, turning it into liquid, passing it through a high-tech filtration system, and then storing it in a tank until the customer is ready to use it. Some of these systems can produce anywhere from 50 to 200 gallons (189 to 757 L) of potable water each day. Right now, they are popular with militaries, but companies are hoping that they gain traction in developing countries where water stress already exists. While the machines do need power in order

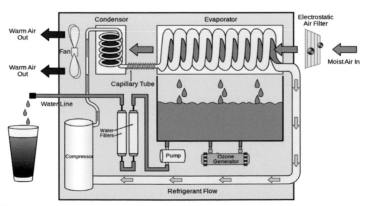

This diagram shows the process of generating water from moist air in the atmosphere.

to run, some are outfitted with solar panels and are essentially self-sufficient.

Cloud Seeding

Some attempts to combat drought are simply more ambitious and have less potential for real-world application than others. Cloud seeding is one of those. This process is a type of weather modification that seeks to affect the amount or type of precipitation that falls from the clouds. In static cloud seeding, a chemical such as silver iodide is spread into the clouds through an airplane or explosives shot into the air from the ground. Moisture can condense around this chemical, which makes rainclouds more effective at raining. Dynamic cloud seeding is similar but tries to boost vertical air currents while the chemical is spread into tropical clouds, essentially "making" more rain. The intent of the cloud-seeding process is to create more rain or snow by physically changing what is happening in the clouds. Though those in favor of cloud seeding hope to drastically increase participation through this innovative technology, the idea has never been proven. During the 2008 Summer

Olympics held in Beijing, city officials did seed the clouds in an attempt to coax rain out before the games. Some have claimed that the methods worked, while many others are skeptical of what exactly can be attributed to the seeding. In early 2018, researchers at the University of Wyoming claimed to have carried out the very first quantifiable observation of cloud seeding. However, it will take many more tests before it is known whether cloud seeding is a viable option for creating precipitation or fighting droughts throughout the world.

Much work is being done by scientists, engineers, climatologists, and others in order to work toward a more drought-resilient world. As long as global warming and climate change affect the planet, there will be more droughts for longer durations, so the goal, for now, must be continued resilience and efforts to lessen the agricultural, economic, environmental, and social impacts that drought and crop failure can have on communities, regions, and the entire world. If it goes unchecked, drought will continue to destroy the crops necessary to feed people and livestock, create biofuel, and do so much more. If crops fail, the reverberations will spread throughout economies, trade relationships, and in the relationships between governments and citizens in unstable countries that could be rocked by major changes in imports, exports, and prices.

Each piece of the drought puzzle is connected. Countless industries will be impacted. Not just farming, but the transportation, utility power, boating, timber, ranching, tractor, and grocery industries will all feel the ill effects of drought and crop failure. Their successes and failures are tied to each other, just like the health, wellness, and success of every person on the planet is bound together. In order to thrive in the future, people must first learn how to survive in the present context that has been created—heat, lack of moisture, and all. It won't be easy, but already some of the world's most brilliant individuals are coming together to brainstorm new and innovative solutions to this very scary and very real problem. Hopefully, the world's citizens can keep collaborating, conserving, researching, and working together to protect ourselves—and our world—from the effects of drought and crop failure.

YOUNG INNOVATOR

Kiara Nirghin proves that climate science has no age requirement.

In 2016, sixteen-year-old Kiara Nirghin of South Africa won the Google Impact Award for her invention of a new polymer to combat drought. Nirghin used orange peel and avocado skins to create a super-absorbent polymer (SAP) that can store massive reserves of water. The material is soil-ready and inexpensive. Her project was chosen from a science fair. She is now working with a Google mentor to further develop the polymer in the hopes that South African farmers can one day utilize it to form reservoirs and help maintain their crops amidst dry conditions.

GLOSSARY

aquifer A geological formation, such as permeable rock, that contains groundwater, often accessed by wells and streams.

climate model A system of computer-driven mathematical equations that helps scientists understand the climate and project changes to the climate.

crop failure The state in which crops do not yield enough food to consume or sell.

drought A period of abnormally low rainfall.

duration Length of time.

famine An extreme shortage of food.

food insecurity A lack of reliable access to enough affordable and nutritious food.

fossil fuel An energy-rich fuel, such as coal or gas, formed through the breakdown of ancient dead organisms.

green Another name for an environmentally friendly plant or product.

principle of common but differentiated responsibilities The acknowledgement that different countries have varied capabilities and responsibilities toward addressing the causes of climate change.

resilient The ability to recover quickly.

xeriscaping The act of forming a landscape that requires little to no irrigation.

Glossary

FURTHER INFORMATION

Books

Ingram, B. Lynn, and Frances Malamud-Roam. *The West Without Water: What Past Floods, Droughts, and Other Climate Clues Tell Us About Tomorrow.* Oakland, CA: University of California Press, 2015.

McGraw, Seamus. *Betting the Farm on a Drought: Stories From the Front Lines of Climate Change.* Austin, TX: University of Texas Press, 2015.

Meister, Cari. *Droughts.* Pogo: Disaster Zone. Minneapolis, MN: Jump! 2016.

Ogden, Scott, and Lauren Springer Ogden. *Waterwise Plants for Sustainable Gardens: 200 Drought-Tolerant Choices for All Climates.* Portland, OR: Timber Press, 2011.

Sneideman, Joshua, and Erin Twamley. *Climate Change: Discover How It Impacts Spaceship Earth*. White River Junction, VT: Nomad Press, 2014.

Websites

Mocomi: What Is a Drought?

http://mocomi.com/what-is-a-drought

This site gives interesting information, fun facts, and resources about drought and climate change.

National Drought Mitigation Center: Drought for Kids

http://drought.unl.edu/DroughtforKids.aspx

This site has explanations, resources, and drought-preparedness plans.

Ready: Drought

https://www.ready.gov/kids/know-the-facts/drought

Here you can get professional tips for preparing for and avoiding natural disasters, as well as what to do when they occur.

SELECTED BIBLIOGRAPHY

Amadeo, Kimberly. "How the Dust Bowl Environmentally Impacted the US Economy: The Scary Thing Is That It Could Happen Again." *The Balance*, December 6, 2017. https://www.thebalance.com/what-was-the-dust-bowl-causes-and-effects-3305689.

"Drought in Kenya Puts Livestock at Risk; Crop Failure Triggers Risk of Starvation." Down to Earth, January 24, 2017. http://www.downtoearth.org.in/news/drought-in-kenya-puts-livestock-at-risk-crop-failure-triggers-fear-of-starvation-56873.

Geiling, Natasha. "Heat Waves and Droughts Are Already Having a Devastating Impact on Important Crops." ThinkProgress, January 7, 2016. https://thinkprogress.org/heat-waves-and-drought-are-already-having-a-

devastating-impact-on-important-crops-
2a756488545d.

Ingram, B. Lynn, and Frances Malamud-Roam.
*The West Without Water: What Past Floods,
Droughts, and Other Climate Clues Tell Us
About Tomorrow.* Oakland, CA: University of
California Press, 2015.

Krajick, Kevin. "In Biblical Land, Searching
for Droughts Past and Future." State of the
Planet: Earth Institute, Columbia University,
October 31, 2017. http://blogs.ei.columbia.
edu/2017/10/31/in-biblical-land-searching-
for-droughts-past-and-future.

Latham, Brian. "South African Drought Slams
Everything From Grapes to Lambs."
Bloomberg, December 20, 2017. https://www.
bloomberg.com/news/articles/2017-12-20/
wine-grapes-to-lambs-squeezed-as-south-
africa-drought-drags-on.

McGraw, Seamus. *Betting the Farm on a
Drought: Stories from the Front Lines of*

Climate Change. Austin, TX: University of Texas Press, 2015.

Monks, Kieron. "16-year-old South African Invents Wonder Material to Fight Drought." CNN, August 14, 2016. https://www.cnn.com/2016/08/09/africa/orange-drought-kiara-nirghin/index.html.

Okiror, Samuel. "Drought Takes Centre Stage in Kenya's Election Campaign as Food Prices Rise." *Guardian*, June 2, 2017. https://www.theguardian.com/global-development/2017/jun/02/drought-centre-stage-kenya-election-campaign-food-prices-rise.

Prisco, Jacopo. "Desert 'Fog Catchers' Make Water Out of Thin Air." CNN, November 18, 2016. https://www.cnn.com/2016/11/18/africa/fog-catchers-morocco/index.html.

Roberts, Rachel. "Pakistan Could Face Mass Droughts by 2025 as Water Level Nears 'Absolute Scarcity'." *Independent*. September 15, 2017. http://www.

independent.co.uk/news/world/pakistan-
droughts-2025-warning-water-
levels-a7949226.html.

Romero, Ezra David. "An Ancient Native
American Drought Solution for a Parched
California." NPR For Central California,
June 2, 2015. http://kvpr.org/post/ancient-
native-american-drought-solution-parched-
california.

Toulmin, Camilla. "Drought and the Farming
Sector: Loss of Farm Animals and Post-
Drought Rehabilitation." ALPAN–African
Livestock Policy Analysis Network, Network
Paper No. 10, September 1986. http://www.
fao.org/wairdocs/ILRI/x5446E/x5446e00.
htm#Contents.

Worland, Justin. "How Climate Change
Unfairly Burdens Poorer Countries." *Time*,
February 5, 2016. http://time.com/4209510/
climate-change-poor-countries.

INDEX

hurricane, 5

hydrological drought, 8–9,
    12, 35, 63

irrigation, 9, 35

meteorological drought, 7,
    9, 12, 35

monsoons, 31–33

no-till farming, 56

precipitation, 5–8, 10, 14,
    23, 48, 66–67

principle of common
    but differentiated
    responsibilities, 26

resilient, 42, 67

socioeconomic drought, 12,
    14, 37

soil, **4**, 7, 9, 11, 20–23, 48,
    54, 56, 62, 64, 69

tornado, 5, 7–8

types of drought, main,
    6–10

water monitoring, 42, 45, **45**

wildfires, 23–24, 38–39

xeriscaping, **51**, 52

ABOUT THE AUTHOR

Kaitlyn Duling believes in the power of words to change hearts, minds, and, ultimately, actions. An avid reader and writer who grew up in Illinois, she now resides in Pittsburgh, Pennsylvania. She loves to learn about and advocate for a healthy, sustainable environment.